B·A·S·I·C S·I·G·N

COMMUNICATION

VOCABULARY

B·A·S·I·C S·I·G·N

COMMUNICATION

William Newell
Chairperson, Communication Training Department
Communication Program, NTID

Frank Allen Paul
Illustrator

Sign Consultants
Samuel Holcomb
Katherine Jankowski
Barbara Ray Holcomb

September, 1983

VOCABULARY

Acknowledgement

Grateful acknowledgement is given to my deaf friends and colleagues, Samuel K. Holcomb, Katherine Jankowski, and Barbara Ray Holcomb, who served as sign consultants to review all illustrations in this book. Thanks are also extended to the entire staff of the Communication Training Department. Without their support and dedicated work over the years, the Basic Sign Communication curriculum of which this book is a part would not have been possible.

Table of Contents

Introduction

This sign dictionary is designed for use by students enrolled in Basic Sign Communication I, II, and III courses developed at the National Technical Institute for the Deaf (NTID) of the Rochester Institute of Technology (RIT) in Rochester, NY. These three courses include approximately 1,000 signs important for everyday conversation, grammatical principles for using these signs, and background information regarding the linguistics of sign language, deaf culture, and education of deaf people in the United States.

This dictionary is divided into three illustrated sections: Sign Vocabulary, Numbers, and Classifiers. The Manual Alphabet is printed on the inside of the back cover. An Index at the end of the dictionary provides a reference to the page numbers on which the illustrations for the sign vocabulary appear.

Signs illustrated in this dictionary were selected for their relevance to basic adult conversational communication. Because the program of sign/simultaneous communication instruction at NTID is designed to prepare individuals for work in an academic environment, some signs are specific to communication in that setting. Most of the vocabulary, however, is relevant to basic conversational needs and can be used in any basic sign course. Basic Sign Communication I, II, and III provide an excellent base for more advanced study in the development of sign communication skills.

Signs in this dictionary are in current usage by skilled American Sign Language (ASL) users. As with all languages, however, ASL undergoes a continuous process of change, with old signs modified and new signs added in accordance with the needs of sign communicators (Bellugi & Newkirk, 1981; Frishberg, 1975). Some of the signs represented here may differ from the signs currently used in your geographical area. A sign instructor should be able to demonstrate some of these variations. Because there may be more than one correct sign for expressing a concept or feeling, a new signer should use those signs which facilitate effective communication. Emphasis should be on the act of communicating rather than the form of the communication. Part of the beauty of human communication is the variety of ways in which people are able to express the same ideas and feelings. This is true for spoken and written communication, as well as sign communication.

A dictionary of signs can not teach sign language. This collection of signs is intended for use by students as they go through a formal course of instruction. It is difficult to represent the depth dimension and movement of a sign in a two dimensional still drawing. Therefore, using this sign dictionary without the guidance of an instructor or without seeking live demonstration of the signs by a skilled sign language communicator could lead to misinterpretation of the sign illustrations. Formal instruction from a qualified teacher is important.

The sign vocabulary section of this dictionary is arranged in alphabetical order according to the first letter of the 'gloss-word'. A gloss has been selected to represent the sign's fundamental meaning. American Sign Language has no popularly accepted written form. This necessitates the use of English words to identify signs in writing. In this dictionary glosses are represented in all capital letters. If two or more English words are needed to identify the fundamental meaning, they are connected by hyphens. See illustrations below for examples of single and multiple word sign glosses:

In many cases, other English words have been identified which can be translated into sign language by the same sign. These additional words are listed in parenthesis next to the primary gloss. This means that it would be appropriate to use the illustrated sign to translate the English words in parenthesis. These references will also be helpful in clarifying the meaning and usage of the sign. See examples below:

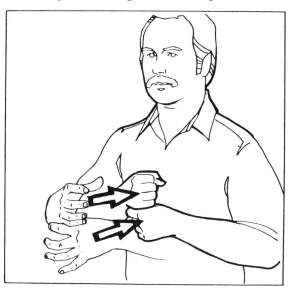

GET (obtain, receive)

NURSE

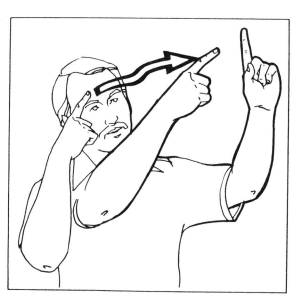

GOAL (aim, objective)

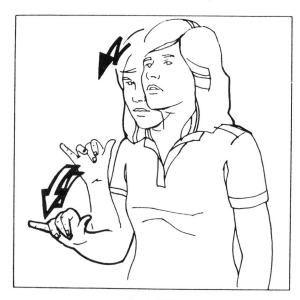

OH-I-SEE

Notice that sometimes the first letter of an associated word is underscored. This indicates that some signers will use this manual alphabet letter as the handshape while producing the sign. In this dictionary, underscoring of initial letters occurs only on words/signs which are frequently initialized by signers to exactly specify these words in English. However, the sign as illustrated, can be used without initialization for all the words in the parenthesis. See examples below:

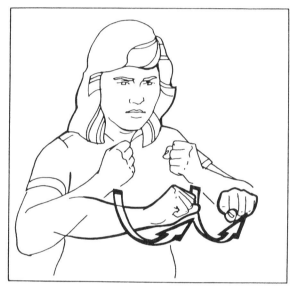

TRY (<u>a</u>ttempt, <u>e</u>ffort, <u>t</u>ry)

WORD (<u>v</u>ocabulary)

Finally, notice that some signs are illustrated showing more than one version. When there is more than one popular way to represent a concept with a sign, each version of the sign is numbered using subscripts. See example below:

BREAKFAST$_1$

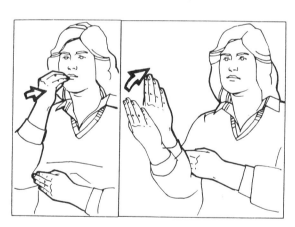

BREAKFAST$_2$

3

Both gloss-words and associated English words are listed in the Index. Gloss-words appear in all capital letters. Associated English words are cross referenced and appear in lower case letters. These words are followed by the gloss-word in parenthesis. For example:

about (APPROXIMATELY)
aim (GOAL)

The Sign Vocabulary section of the dictionary is arranged alphabetically according to gloss-words. When looking for the gloss-word for a particular English word, look first in the Index. If the English word is not listed, think of some other English word that means approximately the same thing and see if it is listed. Always cross check with your instructor regarding the sign to use for English words not listed in the Index.

We are pleased that you have an interest in learning sign language. We hope this dictionary will assist you as a reference book for sign vocabulary as you pursue your study.

Production Team

Instructional Developer	- Marsha Young
Media Specialist	- Shirley Loeffler-Wallace
Assistant Media Specialist	- Stephanie Bauer
Designer	- Sharon Monaghan
Phototypographer	- Sarah Perkins

Sign Models

Keitha Boardman

Thelma Bohli

Barbara Ray Holcomb

Samuel Holcomb

Kathy Jankowski

Paul Johnston

William Newell

Donna Pocobello

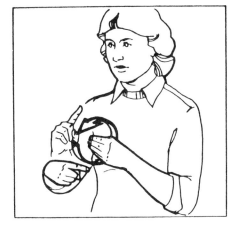

ABOUT

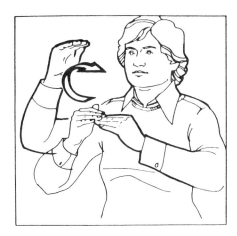

ABOVE

ABSENT (gone)

ACCEPT

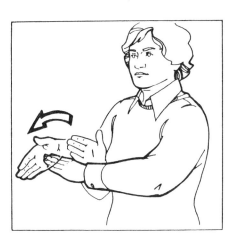

ACROSS (over)

ACT (drama, perform, theatre)

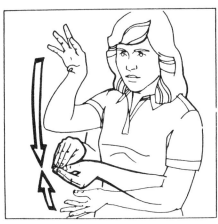

ADD (total, add up)

ADDRESS (live)

7

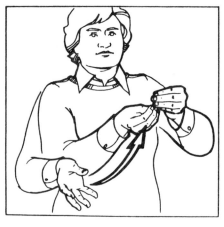

ADD-TO (extra)

ADMIT (confess)

ADVISE (advice, counsel)

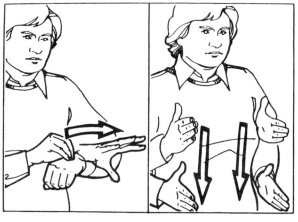

ADVISOR (counselor)

AFFORD (debt)

AFRAID (fear)

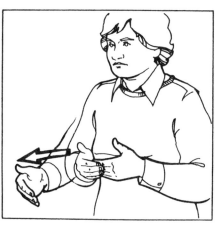

AFTER

AFTERNOON

8

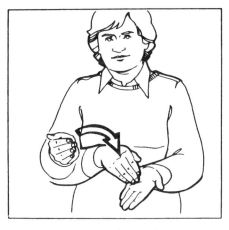

AGAIN (repeat)

AGAINST

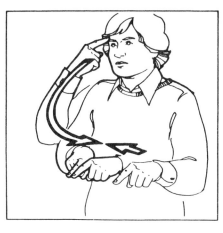

AGREE

AHEAD

AIRPLANE (airport)

ALGEBRA

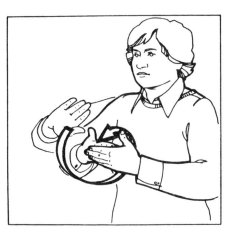

ALL

ALL-AFTERNOON

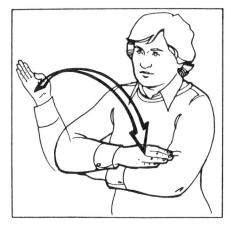

ALL-DAY

9

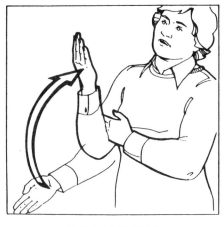

ALL-MORNING

ALL-NIGHT

ALL-RIGHT

ALLOW (let, permit)

ALMOST

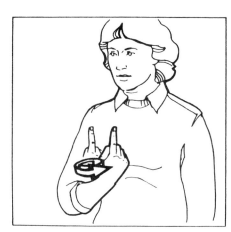

ALONE

A-LOT (much)

ALPHABET

ALPHABET-LETTER (letter)

ALWAYS

AM₁

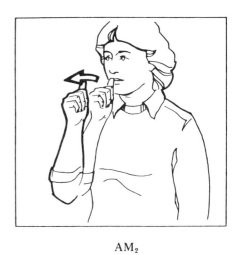

AM₂

AMONG

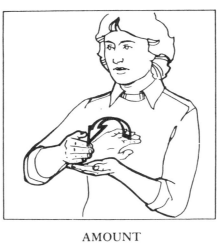

AMOUNT

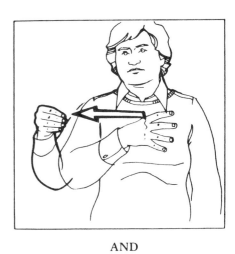

AND

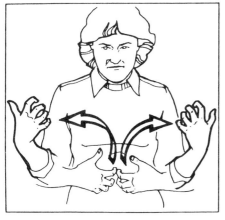

ANGRY

ANSWER

ANY

11

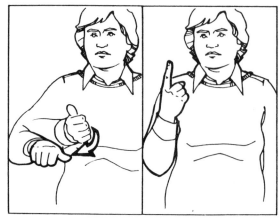

ANYONE

APARTMENT

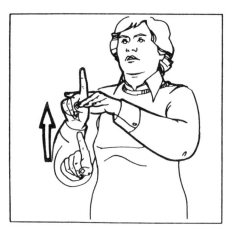

APPEAR (show up)

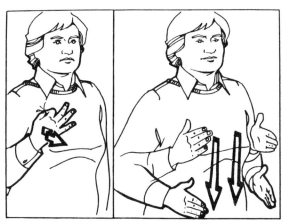

APPLICANT (volunteer, candidate)

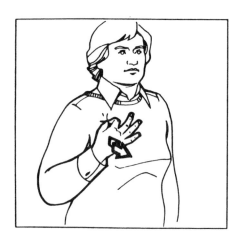

APPLY (volunteer)

APPOINTMENT

APPROXIMATELY (about)

12

ARE₁

ARE₂

AREA₁

AREA₂

ARGUE

ARRIVE (get to)

ARTICLE (column)

ASHAME

ASK (question)

13

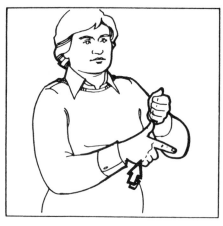

ASSISTANT

ASSOCIATE (each other)

ATTEND (go to)

ATTEND-REGULARLY (attendance)

AUNT

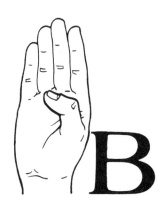

BABY

BACON

14

BAD

BASEBALL

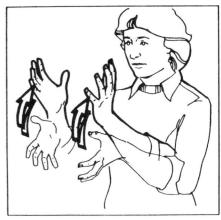

BASKETBALL

BATHROOM (toilet)

BE₁

BE₂

BEAT-COMPETITION (defeat)

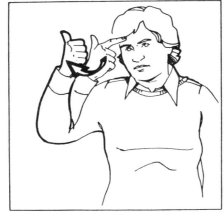

BECAUSE

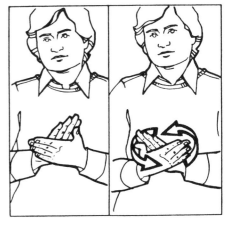

BECOME (get)

15

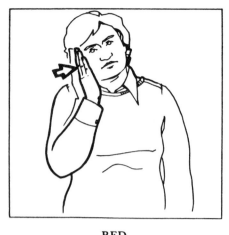

BED

BEER

BEFORE

BEHIND

BELIEVE

BELOW

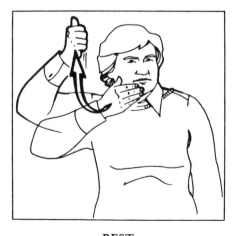

BEST

BETTER

BETWEEN

BICYCLE

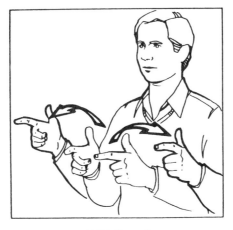

BIG (large)

BIOLOGY

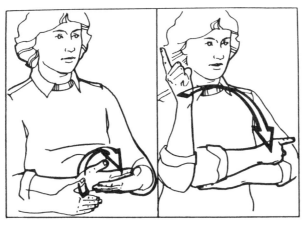

BIRTHDAY

BLACK

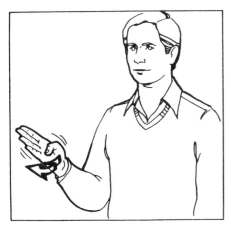

BLUE

BOAT

BODY

17

BOOK

BORING (bored)

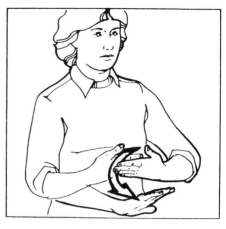

BORN₁ (birth)

BORN₂ (birth)

BORROW

BOSS (chairperson, captain)

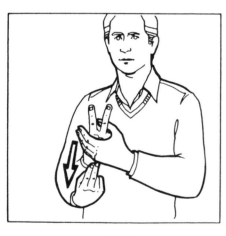

BOTH

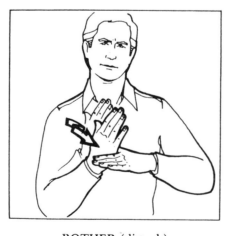

BOTHER (disturb)

BOY

18

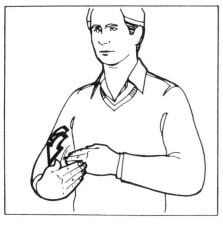

BREAD

BREAK

BREAKFAST₁

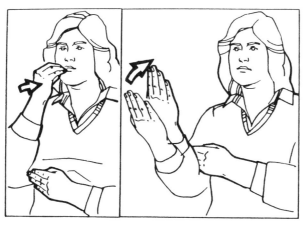

BREAKFAST₂

BRIDGE

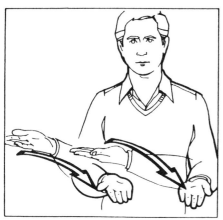

BRING-TO (carry)

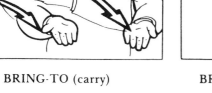

BROKE (busted, without money)

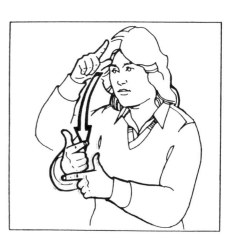

BROTHER₁

19

BROTHER₂

BROWN

BUFFALO-N.Y.

BUILD (building)

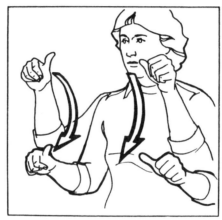

BULLETIN-BOARD (poster)

BUS

BUSY

BUTTER

BUY

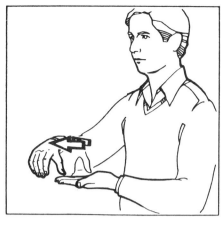

CAKE

CALCULUS

CALL-BY-PHONE (telephone)

CAN

CANCEL (criticize, correct)

CANDY₁

CANDY₂

CAN'T

21

 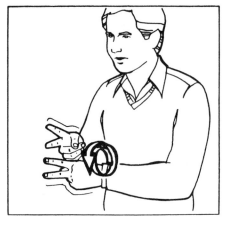 

CAR (drive, automobile)   CAREFUL   BE-CAREFUL

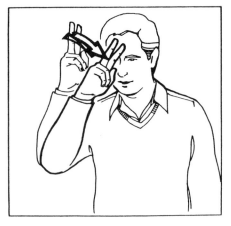 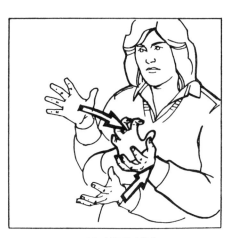 

CARELESS   CATCH-BALL   CATCH-UP

 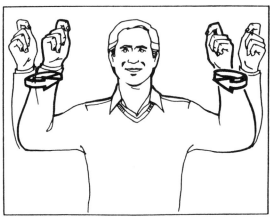

CAUSE (make)   CELEBRATE (anniversary)

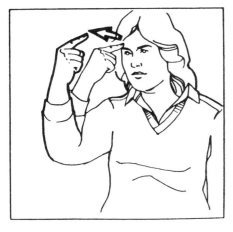

CENT-1 (penny, one cent)

CENT-5 (nickel, five cents)

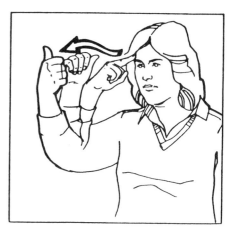

CENT-10 (dime, ten cents)

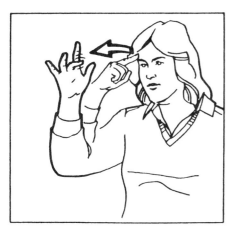

CENT-25 (quarter, twenty-five cents)

CENT-50 (half-dollar, fifty cents)

CERTIFICATE

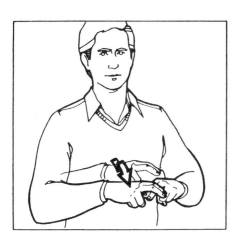

CHAIR (seat)

CHALLENGE

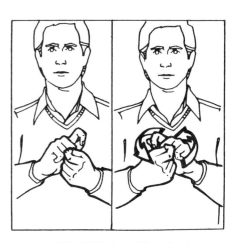

CHANGE (modify, alter)

23

CHARGE (to use credit card)

CHASE

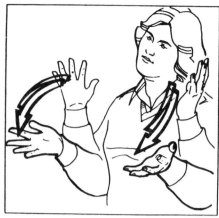

CHAT

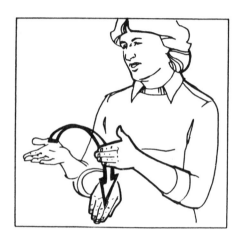

CHEAP (bargain)

CHEAT

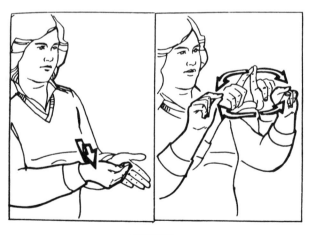

CHECK

CHEMISTRY

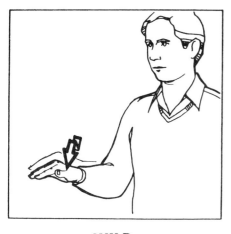

CHILD

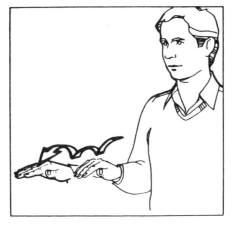

CHILDREN

CHOOSE (pick, sample, select)

CITY (town)

CLASS (group)

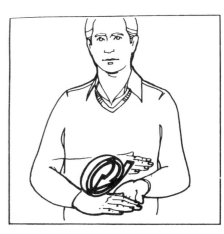

CLEAN-UP

CLEAR (obvious)

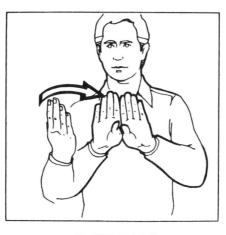

CLOSE-DOOR

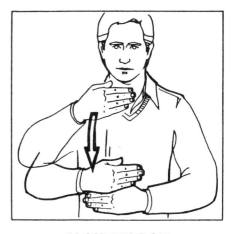

CLOSE-WINDOW

25

COFFEE

COIN

COLD

COLLECT

COLLEGE (university)

COLOR

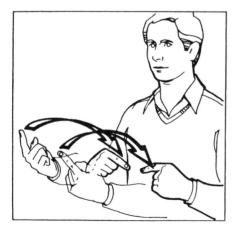

COME

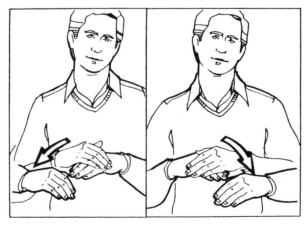

COMFORTABLE

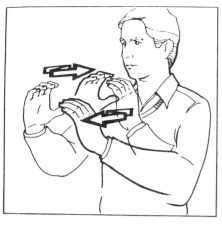

COMMUNICATE

COMMUTE (back and forth)

COMPARE

COMPETE (race)

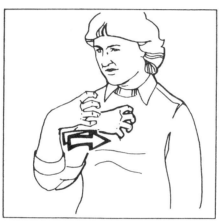

COMPLAIN

COMPUTER

CONFLICT

CONFUSE

CONNECT
(join together, relate, belong)

27

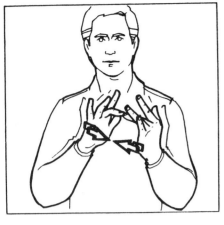

CONTACT

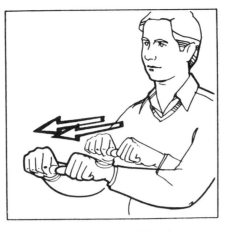

CONTINUE (last)

CONTROL
(manage, run, direct, administrate)

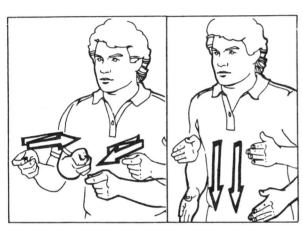

CONTROLLER
(manager, administrator, director)

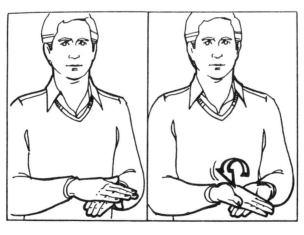

COOK

COOL

28

COOPERATE

COPY (imitate)

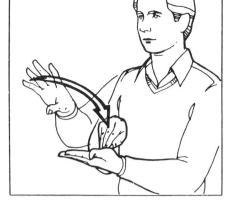

CORNER

COST (charge, price, tax)

COUNT (accounting)

COUNTRY₁

COUNTRY₂

COURSE

COUSIN

29

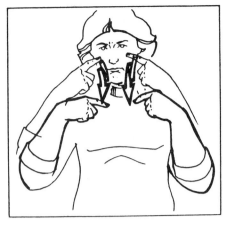

CRY

CURIOUS

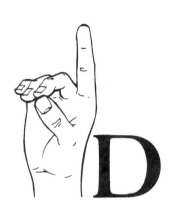

D

DANCE

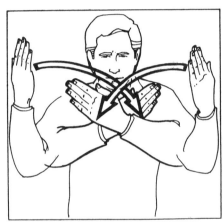

DARK

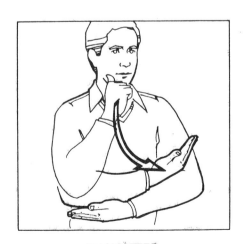

DAUGHTER

DAY

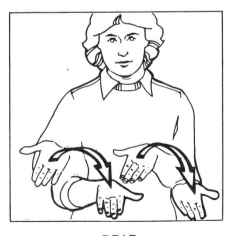

DEAD

DEAF₁

DEAF₂

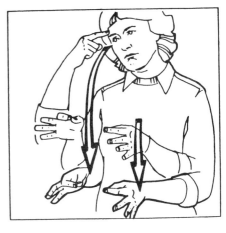

DECIDE

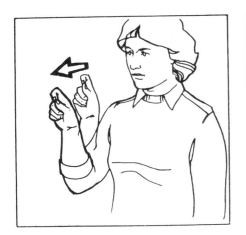

DECIMAL-POINT (decimal)

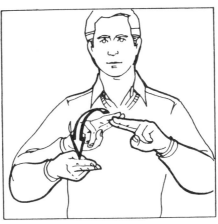

DECREASE (reduce)

DEFEAT (beat, conquer)

DELICIOUS

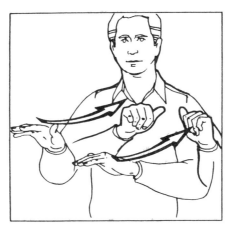

DEPART (leave)

DEPEND-ON

31

DEPOSIT (down payment)

DEPRESSED

DESTROY

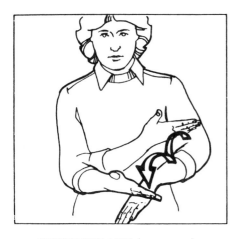

DETERIORATE (get worse)

DICTIONARY

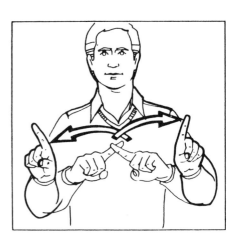

DIFFERENT (but)

DIFFICULT (hard)

DINNER₁

DINNER₂

DIPLOMA₁ (degree)

DIPLOMA₂

DIRECTIONS

DIRTY

DISAGREE

DISAPPEAR

DISAPPOINT (miss)

DISCUSS (debate)

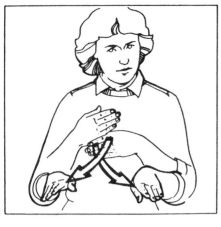

DIVIDE (split)

DIVORCE

DO (act, activity)

DOCTOR₁

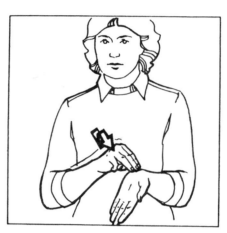

DOCTOR₂

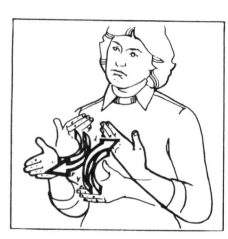

DOESN'T-MATTER
(anyway, nevertheless, regardless)

DOLLAR (bill, paper money)

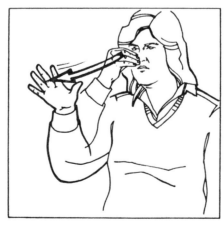

DON'T-CARE₁

DON'T-CARE₂

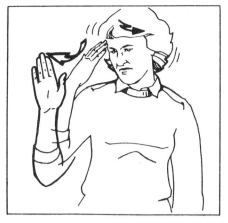

DON'T-KNOW

DON'T-LIKE (dislike)

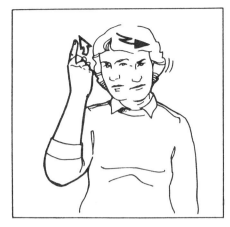

DON'T-UNDERSTAND

DON'T-WANT

DOOR

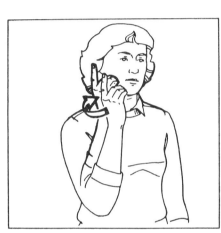

DORM

DOUBT (hesitate)

DRAWER

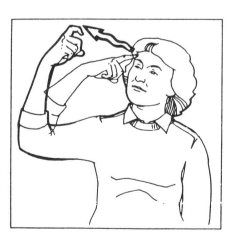

DREAM

35

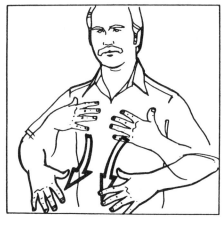

DRESS (clothes)

DRINK

DRIVE-TO

DROP

DURING (while)

E

EACH (every)

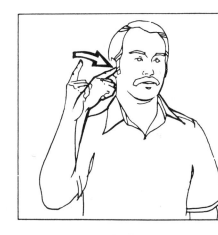

EAR

EARLY

EARN

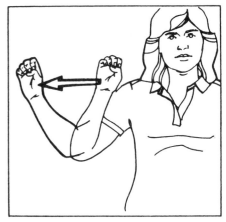

EAST

EASY

EAT (food)

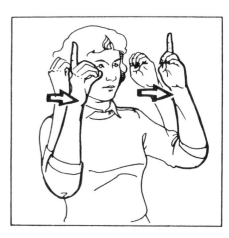

EDUCATION

EGG

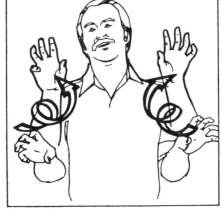

ELABORATE (decorative, fancy)

ELECTRICITY

ELEVATOR

EMBARRASS

EMOTION

EMPTY (bare, blank)

ENGLISH

ENCOURAGE (motivate)

END (complete)

ENJOY (appreciate)

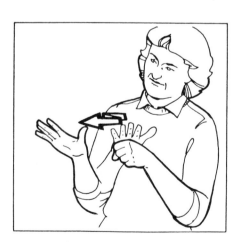

ENOUGH (plenty, sufficient)

ENTER (go into)

ENTHUSIASTIC (motivated)

EQUAL (even, fair)

EQUIPMENT

-ER

ERASE-BOARD

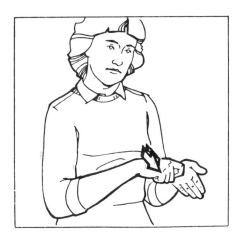

ERASE-PENCIL

ESCAPE (run away, get away)

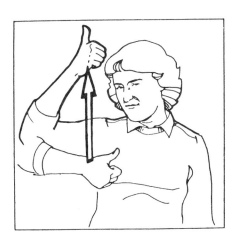

-EST

39

ESTABLISH

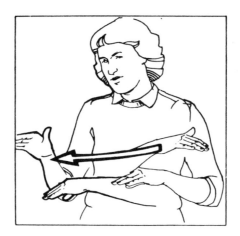

EVERY-AFTERNOON

EVERYDAY (daily)

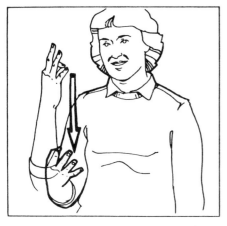

EVERY-FRIDAY (Fridays)

EVERY-MONDAY (Mondays)

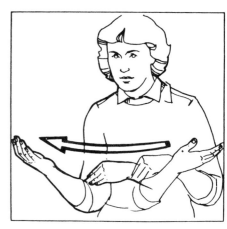

EVERY-MORNING

EVERY-MONTH (monthly, months)

EVERY-NIGHT (nightly)

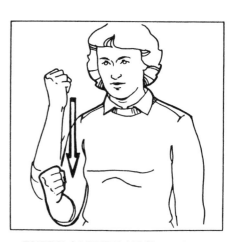

EVERY-SATURDAY (Saturdays)

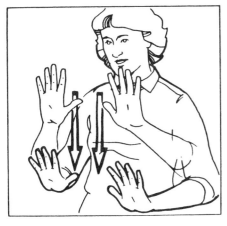

EVERY-SUNDAY (Sundays)

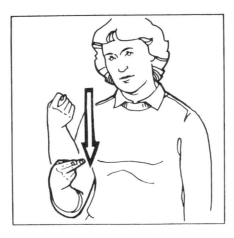

EVERY-THURSDAY (Thursdays)

EVERY-TUESDAY (Tuesdays)

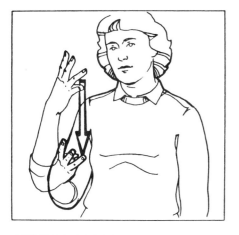

EVERY-WEDNESDAY (Wednesdays)

EVERY-WEEK (weekly, weeks)

EVERY-YEAR (annually, yearly, years)

EXACTLY (precise, perfect)

EXCITE

EXCUSE (forgive, pardon)

41

EXERCISE (gym)

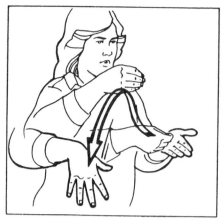

EXPENSIVE

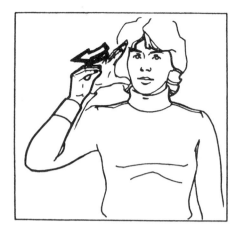

EXPERIENCE

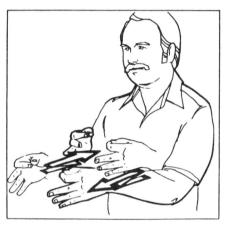

EXPLAIN
(describe, directions, define)

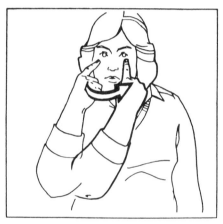

EYES

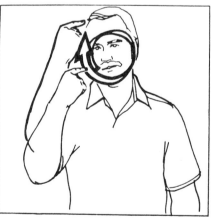

FACE (appearance, looks)

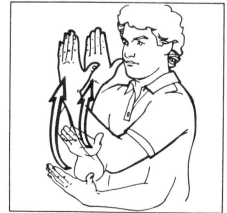

FACE-TOWARD (in front of)

FAIL

FALL (autumn)

FALL-BEHIND

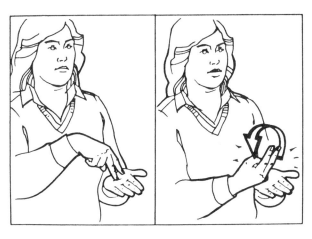

FALL-DOWN

FALSE

FAMILY

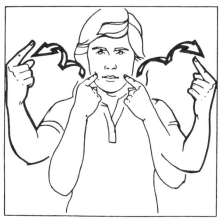

FAMOUS

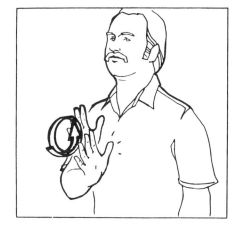

FANCY (formal)

43

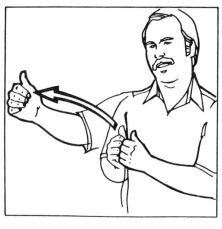

FAR

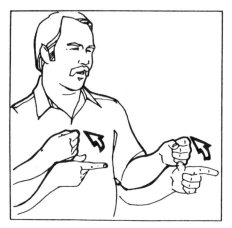

FAST (quick, speed)

FAT

FATHER

FAVORITE

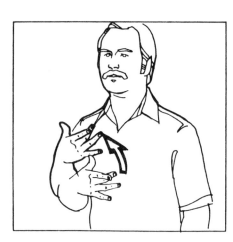

FEEL (emotion, feeling)

FEW (several)

TO-FIGURE (math, arithmetic)

44

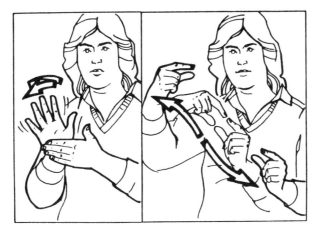

FILM-STRIP

FILES

FIND (discover)

FINE

FINGERSPELL (spell)

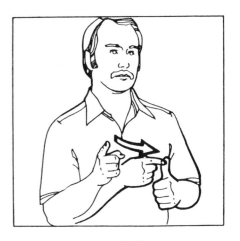

FINISH (have)

FIRE-FROM-JOB

FIRST

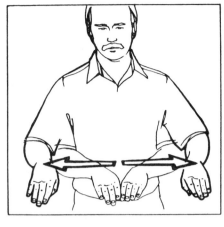  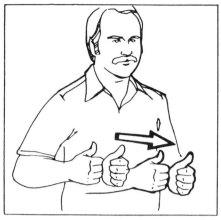

FLOOR   FLY   FOLLOW

FOOTBALL   FOR   FORGET

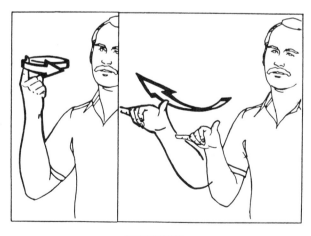 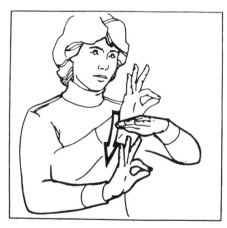

FOREVER   FRACTION

46

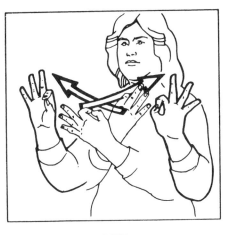

FREE

FRENCH-FRIES

FRESHMAN

FRIDAY

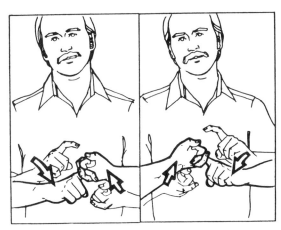

FRIEND

FRIENDLY (pleasant)

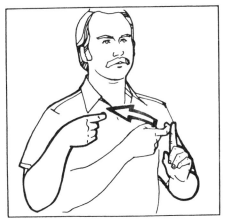

FROM

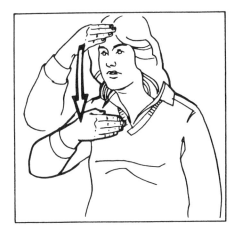

FRONT

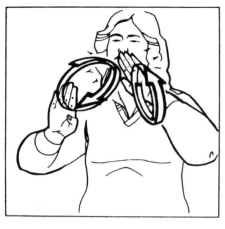

FRUSTRATE

FULL (complete)

FUN

FUNNY

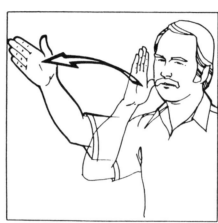

FUTURE (will)

G

GALLAUDET

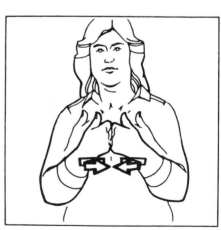

GAME

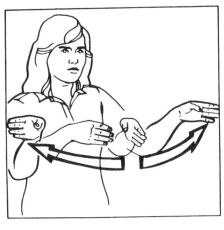

GENERAL

GEOMETRY

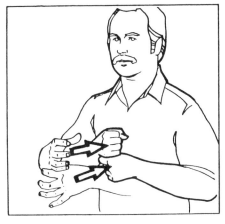

GET (obtain, receive)

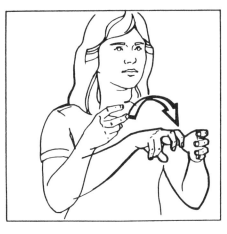

GET-IN

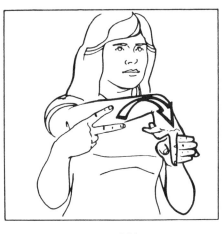

GET-ON

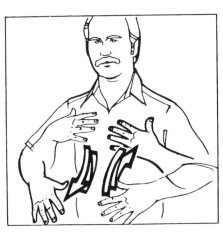

GET-DRESSED

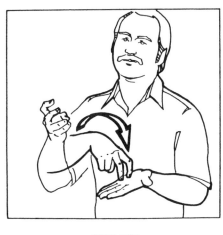

GET-UP

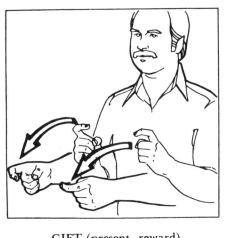

GIFT (present, reward)

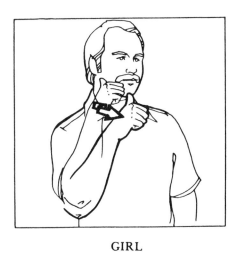

GIRL

GIVE-TO (contribution)

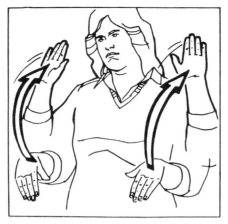

GIVE-UP

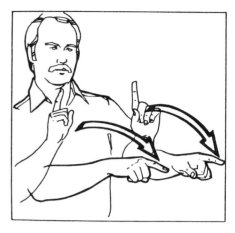

GO

GOAL (aim, objective)

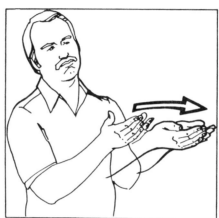

GO-BY-BOAT

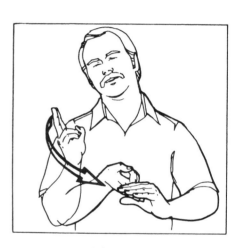

GO-TO-BED

GOOD (well)

GOSSIP

GRADUATE

GRADUATE-SCHOOL

GRANDFATHER

GRANDMOTHER

GREEN

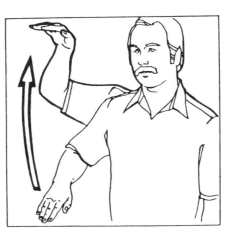

GROW-UP (raised)

GUESS

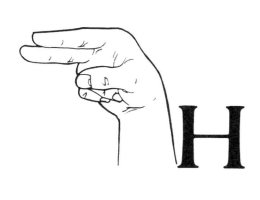

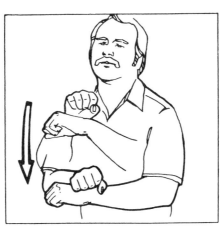

HABIT
(custom, used to, accustomed to)

51

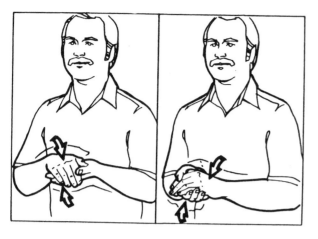

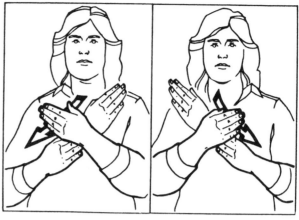

HAMBURGER

HANDS

HAND-TO (give)

HAPPEN (occur)

HAPPY

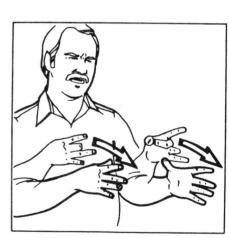

HARD-OF-HEARING

HARD-SOLID (solid)

HATE

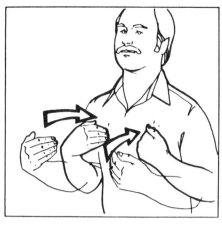

HAVE

HE/SHE/IT

HEAD

HEAD-COLD

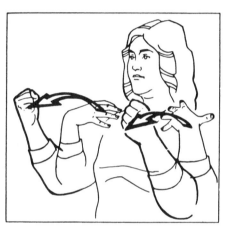

HEALTHY (well)

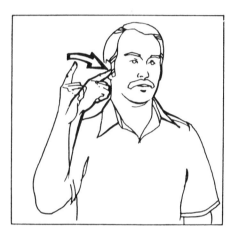

HEAR

HEARING-AID

HEARING-PERSON (say)

HEART

53

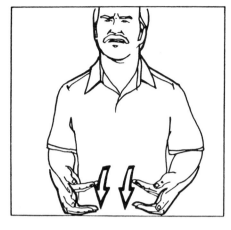

HEAVY

HELP

HERE

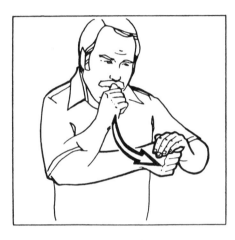

HIDE

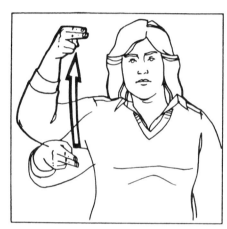

HIGH

HIGH-SCHOOL

HIRE (invite, welcome)

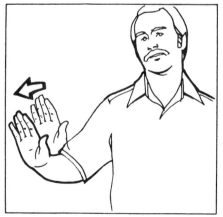

HIS/HERS

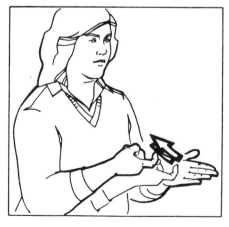

HOCKEY

HOME

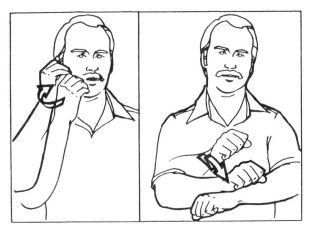

HOMEWORK

HONEST (truth)

HOPE

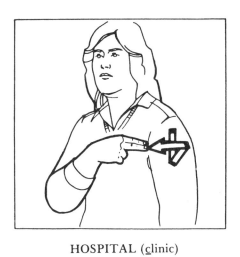

HOSPITAL (clinic)

HOT

HOUR₁

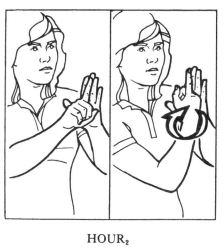

HOUR₂

55

HOUSE

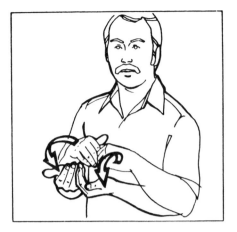

HOW

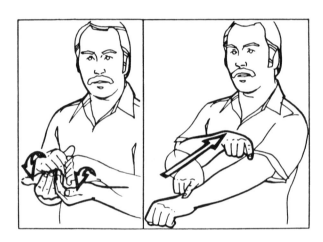

HOW-LONG

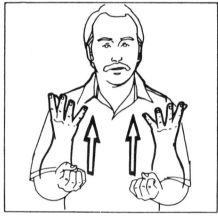

HOW-MANY

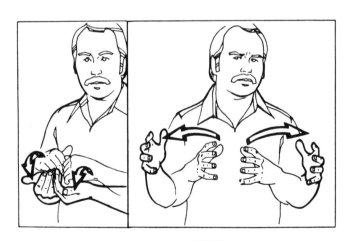

HOW-MUCH

HUNGRY (wish)

56

HURRY (rush)

HURT

HUSBAND₁

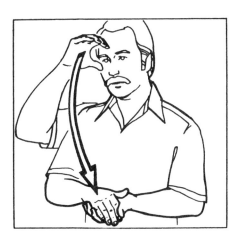

HUSBAND₂

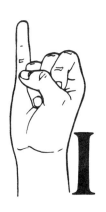

ICE-CREAM

IDEA

57

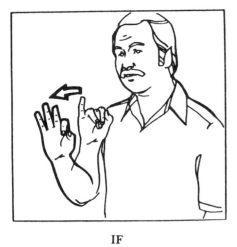

IF

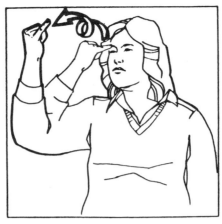

IMAGINE

IMPORTANT (value, worth)

IMPOSSIBLE

IMPROVE (get better)

IN (inside)

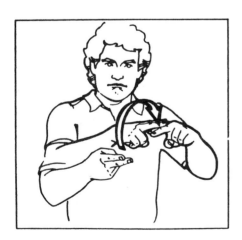

INCREASE (gain)

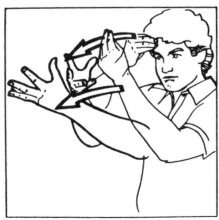

INFORM (let one know, notify)

INSURANCE

58

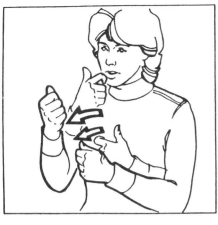

INTERESTED

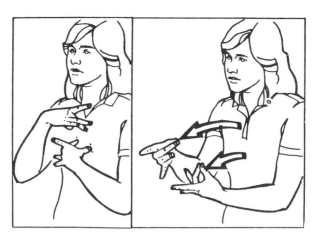

INTERESTING

INTERPRET

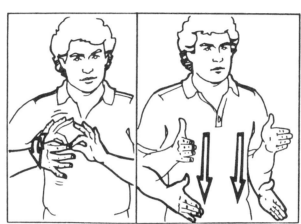

INTERPRETER

INTERRUPT (interfere)

INTERVIEW

IS₁

59

IS₂

JEALOUS

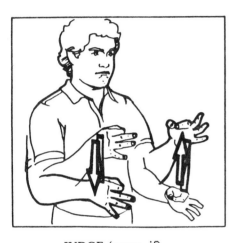

JUDGE (court, if)

JUMP

JUNIOR

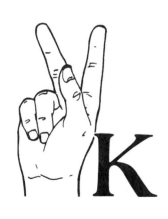

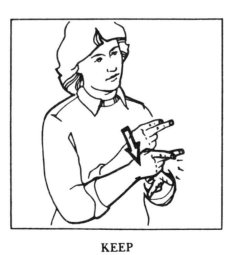

KEEP

KEY

60

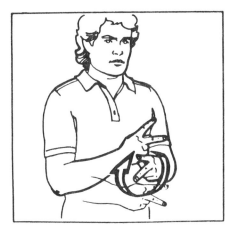

KICK (kick out)

KIND (gentle)

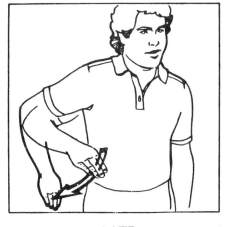

KIND-OF

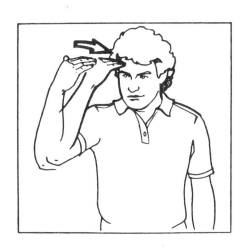

KNOW (aware)

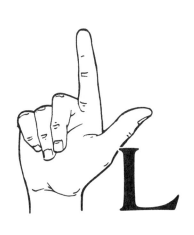

LAST (final)

LATE

61

LATER (after a while)

LAUGH

LAW

LAZY

LEAD

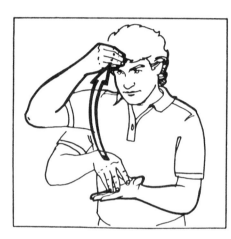
LEARN

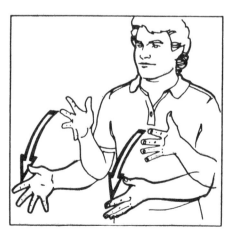
LEAVE

LECTURE (speech)

LEFT-DIRECTION

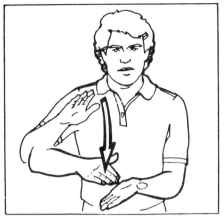
LESS (reduce)

LESSON (chapter, module, unit)

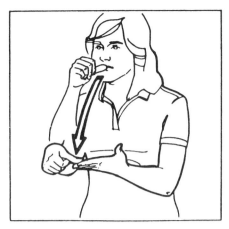
LETTER (mail)

LIBRARY

LICENSE

LIE

LIE-DOWN

LIGHT

LIGHT-BULB

LIGHT-WEIGHT

LIKE

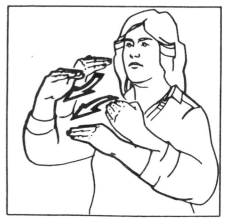

LIMIT

LINE-OF-WORK
(major, field, profession)

LINE-UP

LIST (outline)

TO-LIST

LISTEN

LITTLE-BIT

LIVE

LOAN

LOCKED

TO-LOCK

LONELY

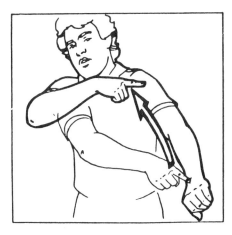

LONG

LONG-AGO

LOOK-AT (watch)

LOOK-FOR (search, hunt)

LOOK-LIKE

LOOK-UP (turn pages)

LOS-ANGELES

LOSE-COMPETITION

LOST

LOUSY

LOVE

LOW₁

LOW₂

LUNCH₁

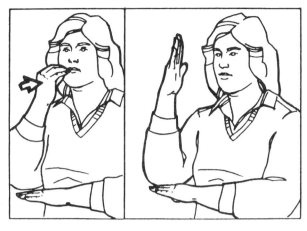

LUNCH₂

MACHINE (mechanical, factory)

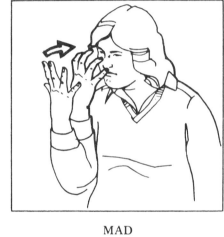

MAD

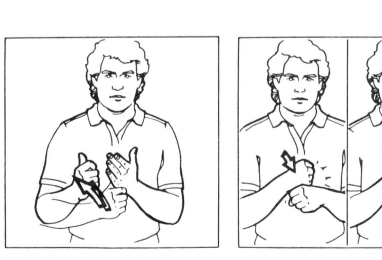

MAGAZINE (pamphlet, brochure)   MAKE

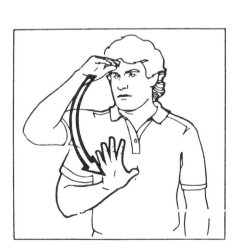

MAN

MANY

MARRY

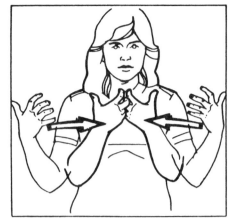

MATCH

MATERIALS

MATH

MAYBE

ME (I)

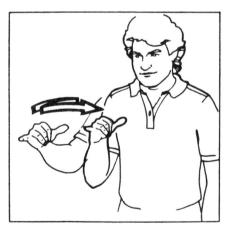

ME-TOO (same as you)

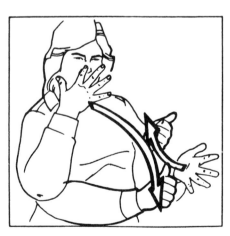

MEAN (cruel)

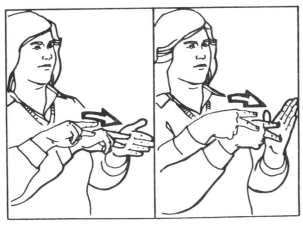 

MEANING (definition) MEASURE (size)

 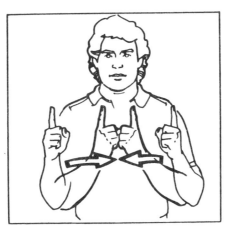 

MEDICINE (medical) MEET MEETING
(conference, convention, session)

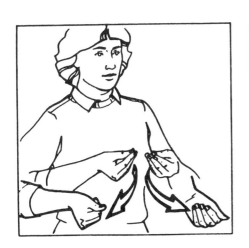 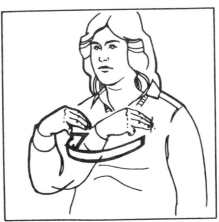 

MELT (dissolve, solve, solution) MEMBER MEMORIZE

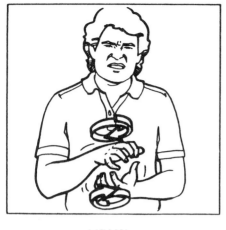

MESSY

MIDDLE (center)

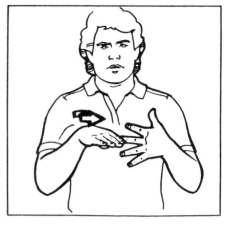

MIDDLE-OF-SERIES

MIDNIGHT

MILK

MINUTE (second)

MISS

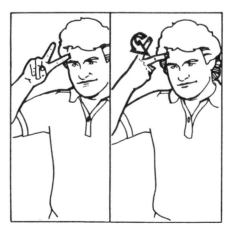

MISUNDERSTAND

MONDAY

MONEY (cash)

MONTH

MONTH-FUTURE (next month)

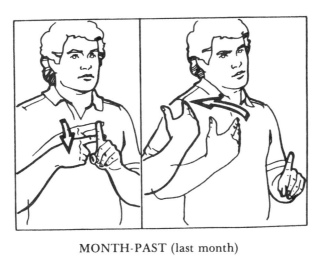

MONTH-PAST (last month)

MORE

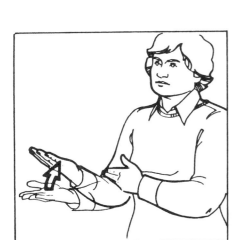

MORNING

MOST

MOTHER

71

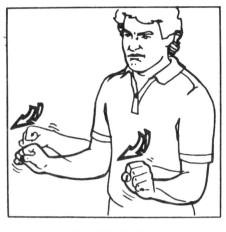

MOTORCYCLE

MOVE

MOVIE (film)

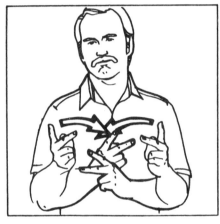

MULTIPLY

MUST (have to, should)

MY (mine)

MYSELF₁ (my own)

MYSELF₂ (my own)

72

N

NAME

NARROW

NATION

NATURAL (usually)

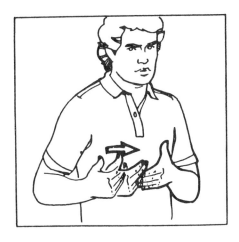

NEAR (close to)

NEED (necessary)

NEIGHBOR

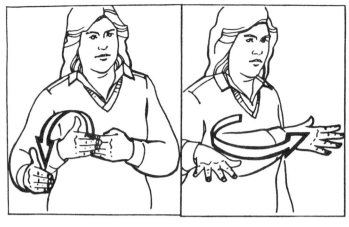

NEIGHBORHOOD

NEGATIVE (minus)

NEPHEW

NERVOUS

NEVER

NEW

NEWSPAPER (print)

NEW-YORK

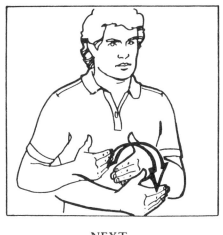

NEXT

NEXT-TO (beside)

NICE (clean, neat)

NIECE

NIGHT

NO

NOISY (noise)

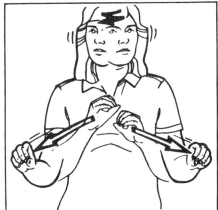

NONE (no)

75

NOON

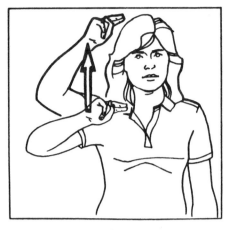

NORTH

NOT (don't, didn't, isn't, wasn't)

NOT-CLEAR (vague)

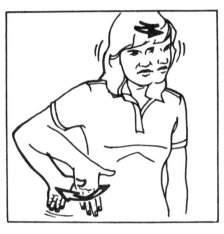

NOT-YET (haven't, yet)

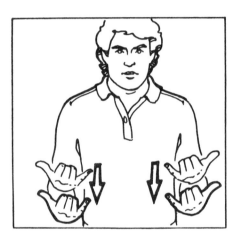

NOW (this)

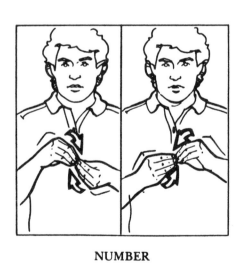

NUMBER

NURSE

OBEY

OFFER (propose, suggest)

OFTEN (frequently)

OH-I-SEE

OK

OLD (age)

OLD-1 (one year old)

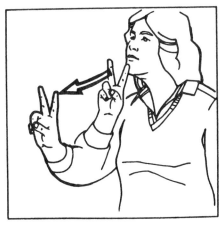

OLD-2 (two years old)

77

OLD-3 (three years old)

OLD-10 (ten years old)

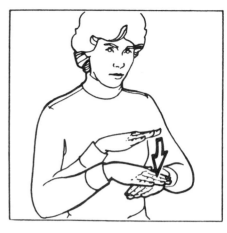

ON

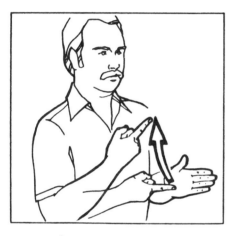

ONCE (single, one time)

1-DOLLAR (first)

OPEN-DOOR

OPEN-WINDOW

OPPORTUNITY

OPPOSITE

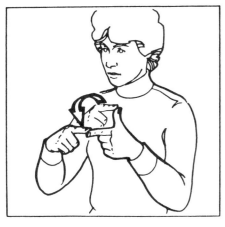

OR (then, second)

ORANGE

ORDER (command)

ORGANIZATION

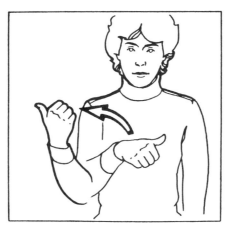

OTHER (else, another)

OUR

OUT (outside)

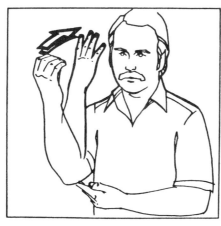

OVERHEAD-PROJECTOR

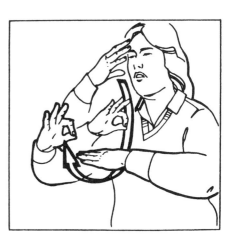

OVERSLEEP

OWE (due)

P

PAIN

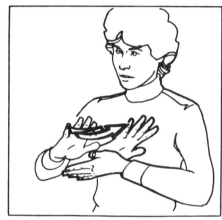

PAPER

PAPER-CLIP

PARAGRAPH

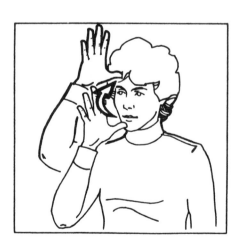

PARENTS₁

80

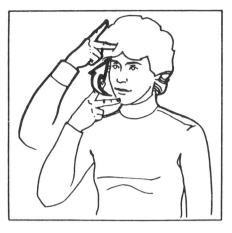

PARENTS₂

PARTICIPATE (join)

PARTY

PASS

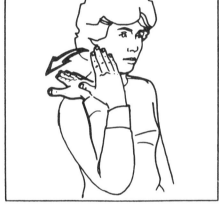

PAST (before, last)

PATHWAY
(street, method, road, way)

PATIENCE

PATIENT

PAY

81

 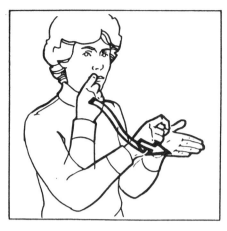 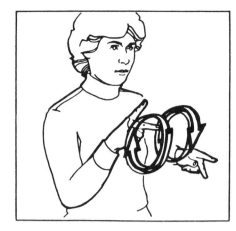

PAY-ATTENTION PENCIL PEOPLE

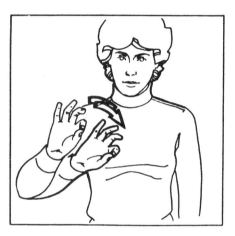  

PEPPER PERCENT PERSON

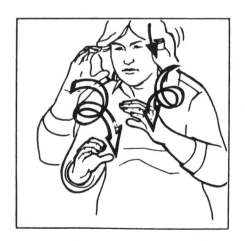  

PHYSICAL-EXAM
(checkup, examination)

PHYSICS PICTURE

PINK

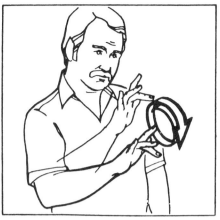

PITY (sympathy)

PLACE (position, location)

PLAIN

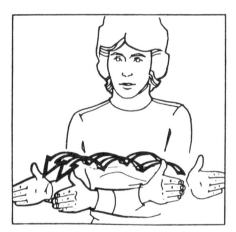

PLAN (prepare)

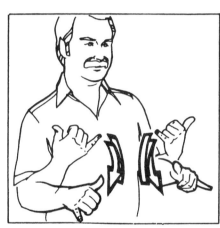

PLAY

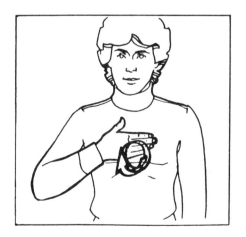

PLEASE

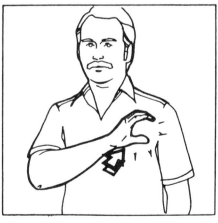

POLICE (cop)

POLICY

83

POOR

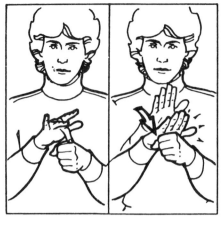

POP (soda)

POPCORN

POSITIVE (plus)

POSSIBLE

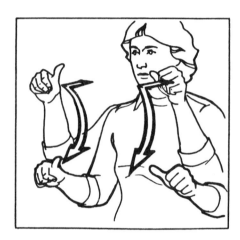

TO-POST

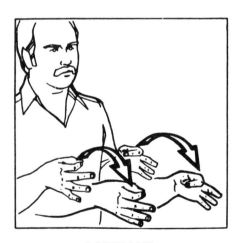

POSTPONE

PRACTICE (train)

PREFER

84

PRETTY (beautiful)

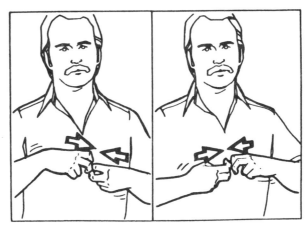

PROBLEM

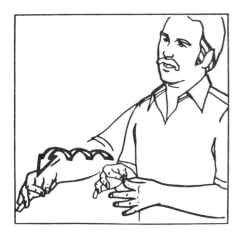

PROCRASTINATE (put off)

PROGRAM

PROJECTOR

PRONOUNCE (pronunciation)

PROUD

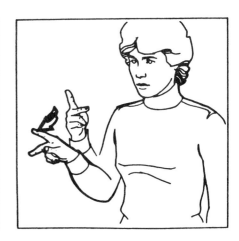

PURPLE

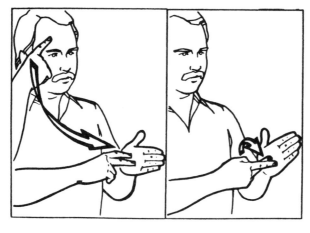

PURPOSE (intend)

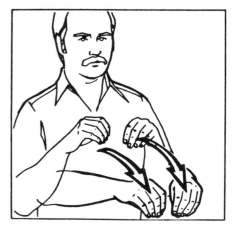

PUT (place)

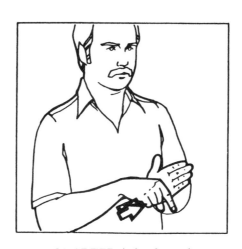

QUARTER (school term)

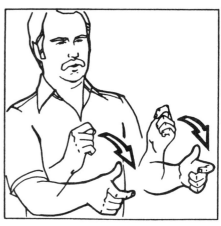

QUICK (fast, immediately)

QUIET (calm, peaceful, still)

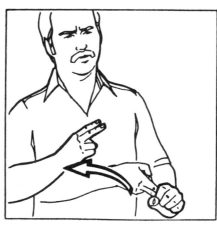

QUIT

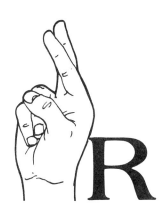
R

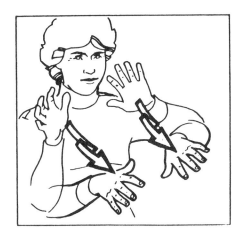
RAIN

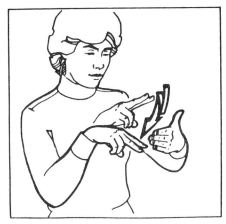
READ

READY

RECENTLY (just)

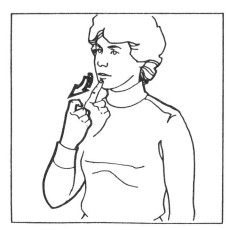
RED

REFUSE (won't)

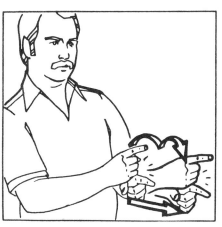
REGULAR

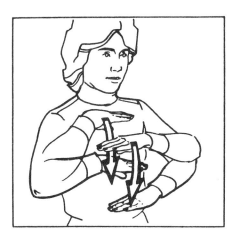
RELIEF

REMEMBER

REMOVE (eliminate)

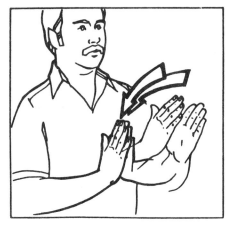

REQUEST (ask)

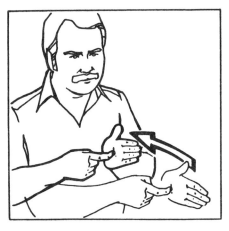

REQUIRE (demand, takes)

RESIDENTIAL-SCHOOL (institution)

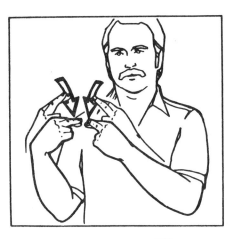

RESPONSIBILITY

REST (relax)

RESTLESS-IN-BED

RESTLESS-SITTING

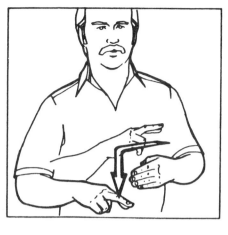

RESULT

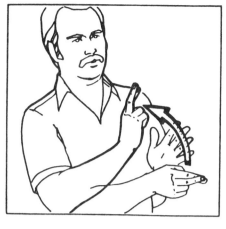

REVIEW

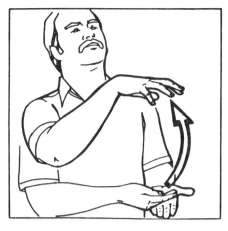

RICH (wealthy)

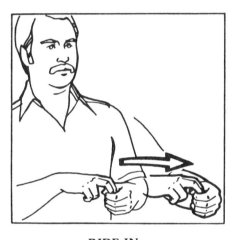

RIDE-IN

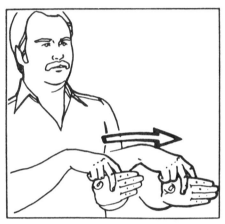

RIDE-ON

RIGHT (correct)

RIGHT-DIRECTION

ROCHESTER

ROOM₁ (box)

89

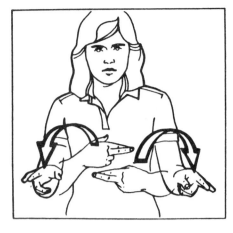

ROOM₂

RUIN (spoil)

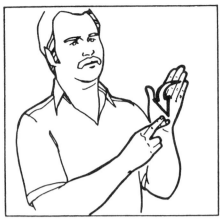

RULE

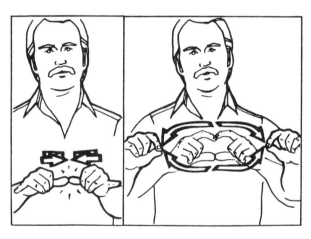

RULER

RUN

S

SAD (unfortunate)

SAFE (free)

SALAD

SALT

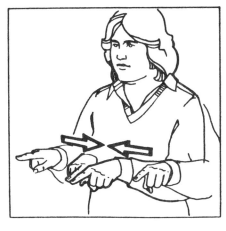

SAME (like, alike, too)

SANDWICH₁

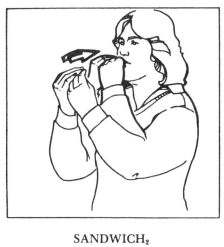

SANDWICH₂

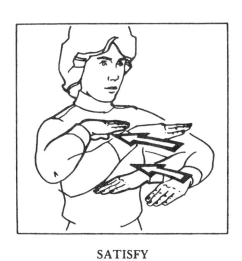

SATISFY

SATURDAY

SAVE (keep)

SAY (hearing person, speak, talk)

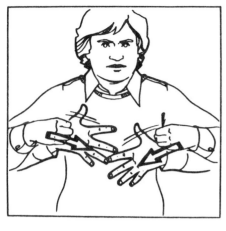

SCARE

SCHEDULE

SCHOOL

SCIENCE (<u>c</u>hemistry, <u>b</u>iology)

SECOND

SECOND-HAND (used)

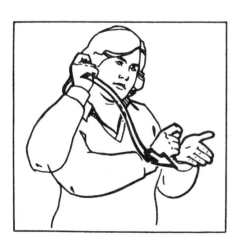

SECRETARY

SEE

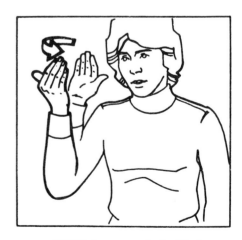

SEEM (appears, looks like)

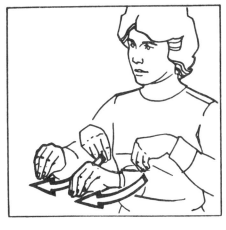

SELL

SEMESTER

SEND (mail)

SENIOR

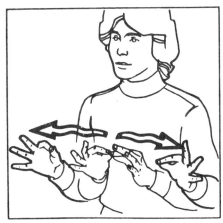

SENTENCE (language, grammar)

SEPARATE

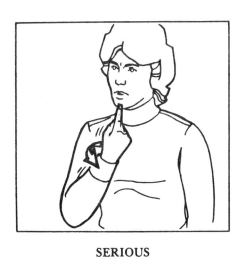

SERIOUS

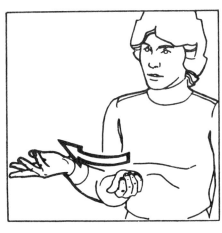

SEVERAL

SHAME

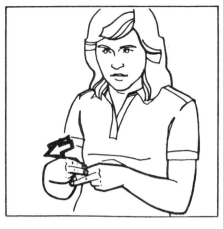

SHORT (soon)

SHORT-STATURE (little)

SHOW (demonstrate)

SHY

SICK (ill)

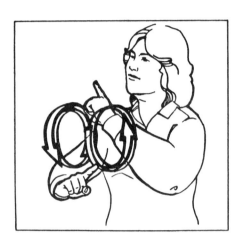

SIGN (sign language)

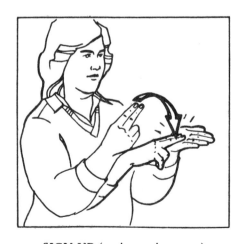

SIGN-UP (register, signature)

SILLY

SIMILAR (same)

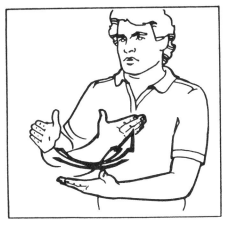

SING (music, song)

SINGLE

SISTER₁

SISTER₂

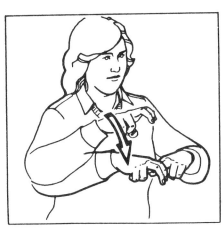

SIT (sit-down)

SKEPTICAL (don't believe, doubt)

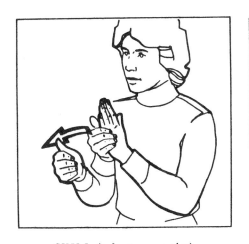

SKILL (talent, expertise)

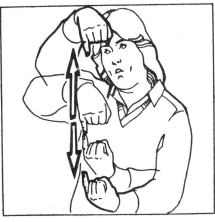

SKINNY

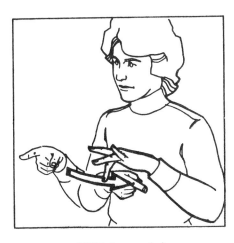

SKIP (cut, miss)

95

SLIDES

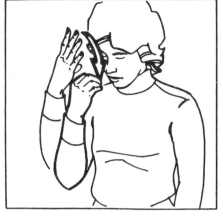

SLEEP

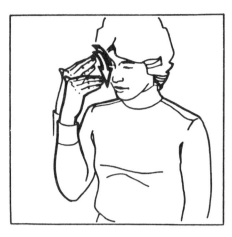

SLEEPY (drowsy)

SLOW

SMALL

SMART (intelligent)

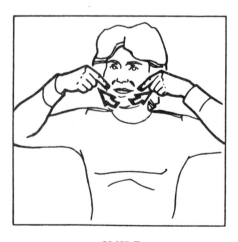

SMILE

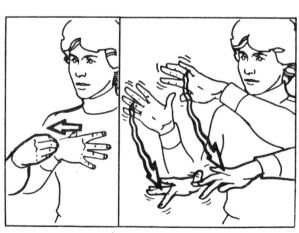

SNOW

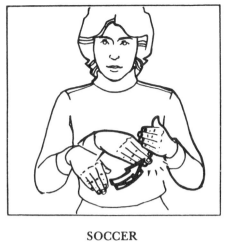

SOCCER

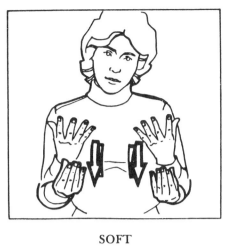

SOFT

SOME (part)

SOMETHING (someone)

SOMETIMES (occasionally)

SON

SOPHOMORE

SORRY (apologize)

SO-SO

SOUP

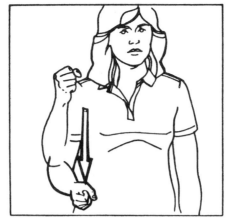

SOUTH

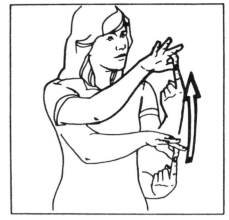
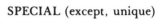

SPECIAL (except, unique)

SPEECH (oral)

SPEECHREAD (lipread)

SPEND

SPRING (grow)

STAIRS

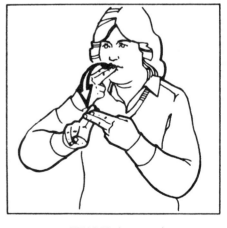

STAMP (postage)

STAND (stand-up)

STAPLER

START (begin)

STATISTICS

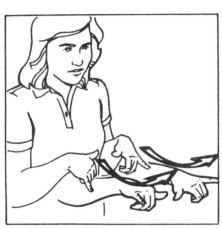

STILL (yet)

STOP

STORE

STORE-AWAY (save, invest)

STORY

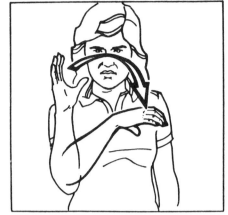

STRANGE

STRONG

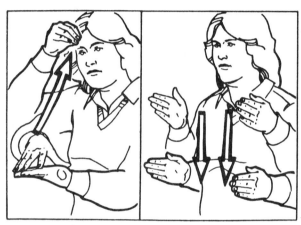

STUDENT

STUDY

STUFFED (full)

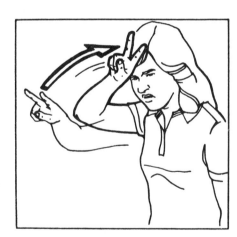

STUPID (ignorant)

SUBTRACT
(deduct, take away from, eliminate)

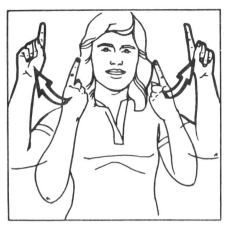

SUCCEED

SUFFER

SUGAR

SUMMARY
(condense, abbreviate)

SUMMER

SUNDAY

SUPERVISE (monitor, take care of)

101

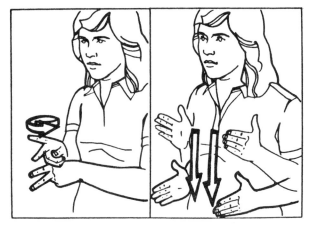

SUPERVISOR

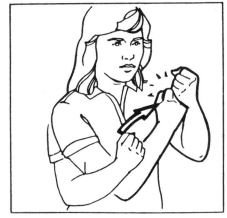

SUPPORT

SUSPECT

SWEETHEART

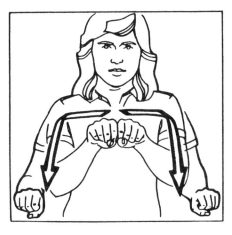

SYSTEM

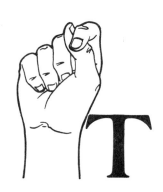

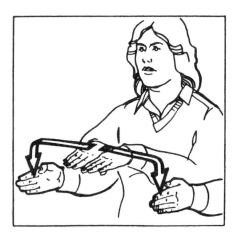

TABLE (desk)

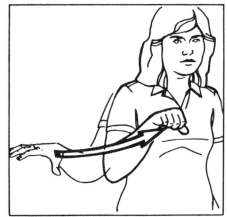

TAKE

TAKE-A-SHOWER

TAKE-UP

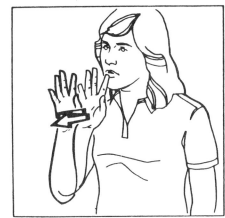

TALK

TALK-WITH (converse)

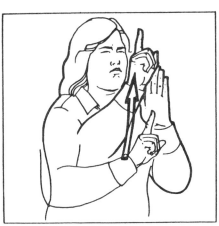

TALL₁

TALL₂

TAPE

TAPE-RECORDER

TASTE

103

TEA

TEACH

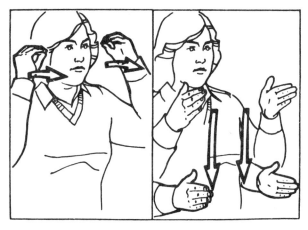

TEACHER

TEAM

TEASE

TECHNICAL (technology)

TELEPHONE (call, phone)

TELL

TEMPERATURE₁ (degrees)

TEMPERATURE₂

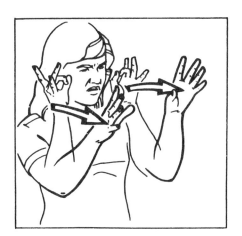

TERRIBLE (awful)

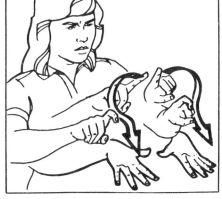

TEST (quiz, exam)

THAN

THANK-YOU (you're welcome)

THAT₁

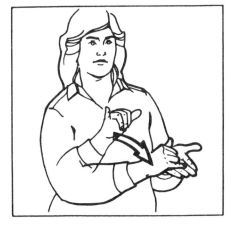

THAT₂

105

THEIR

THESE₁

THESE₂

THEY (those, them)

THICK

THIN₁

THIN₂

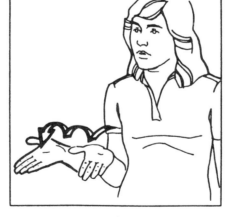

THING (materials, equipment)

THINK

106

THINK-ABOUT (wonder)

THIRSTY

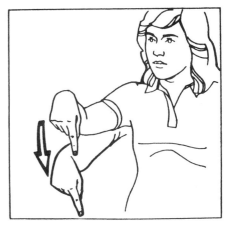

THIS₁

THIS₂

THOSE₁

THOSE₂

THOSE-3

THOSE-2

3-TIMES (triple)

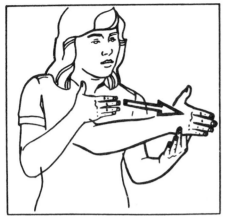

THROUGH

THURSDAY

TICKET

TIME (o'clock)

TIRED

TITLE (quote, subject, topic)

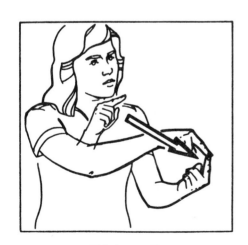

TO (toward)

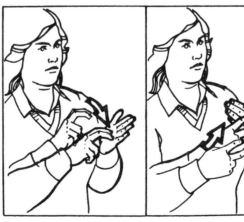

TOAST

TODAY

TOMORROW

TOO-MUCH

TOUCH

TRADE₁ (exchange, substitute)

TRADE₂

TRAIN

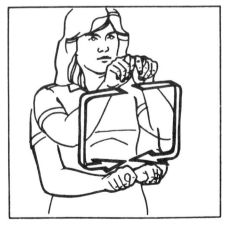

TRANSPARENCY

109

TRAVEL (tour, trip)

TRIGONOMETRY

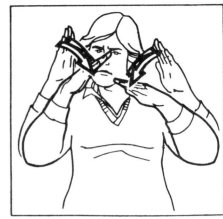

TROUBLE

TRUE

TRY (attempt, effort, try)

TTY

TUESDAY

TURN-LEFT

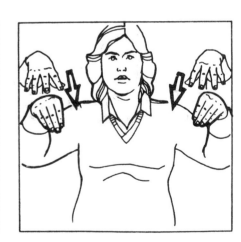

TURN-OFF-LIGHT

110

TURN-ON-LIGHT

TURN-RIGHT

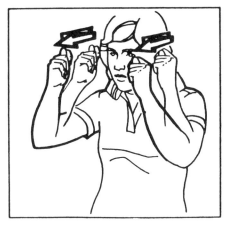

TO-TUTOR

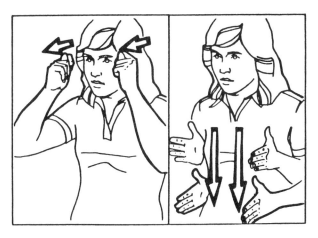

TUTOR

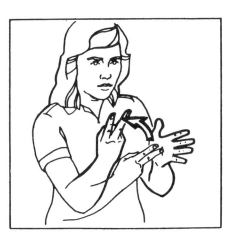

TWICE (double, two times)

TWINS

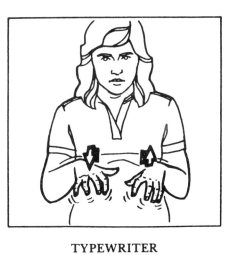

TYPEWRITER

UGLY   UNCLE

  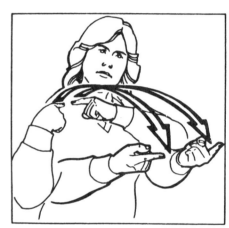

UNDER   UNDERSTAND   UP-TILL-NOW (have been, since)

UPSET   UNTIL (toward)   USE (wear)

VACATION (time off, off)

VALUE (worth, price)

VARIETY (various)

VARY

VISIT

 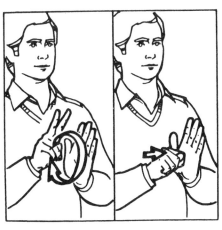

VOICE

VIDEOTAPE

113

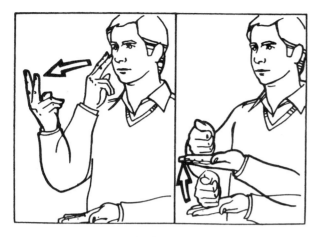

VISUAL-AID

WAIT

WAKE-UP

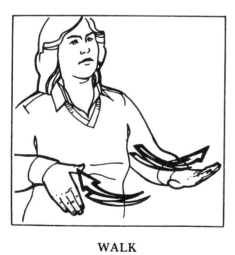

WALK

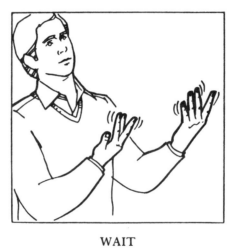

WANT

WARM

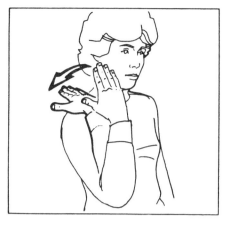

WAS₁

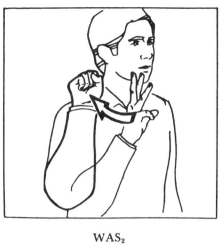

WAS₂

WASH

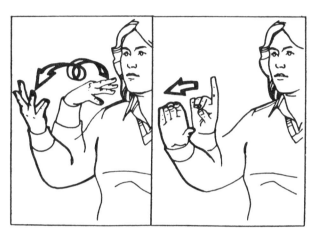

WASHINGTON-D.C.

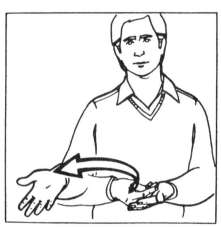

WASTE

WATER

WE (us)

WE-3

WE-2

WEAK

WEATHER

WEDNESDAY

WEEK

WEEK-FUTURE (next week)

WEEK-PAST (last week)

116

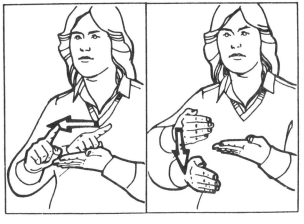

WEEKEND WEIGH (pound, weight)

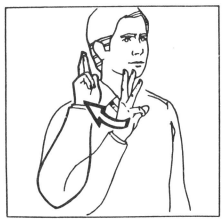

WERE₁ WERE₂ WEST

WHAT WHEN WHERE

WHICH

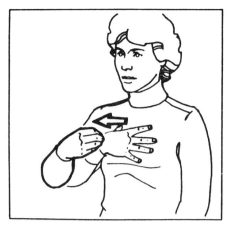

WHITE

WHO₁

WHO₂

WHY

WIDE

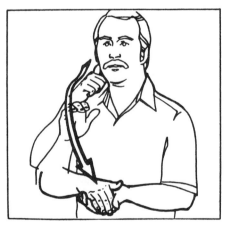

WIFE₁

118

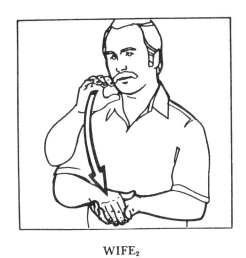

WIFE₂

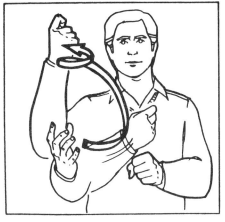

WIN

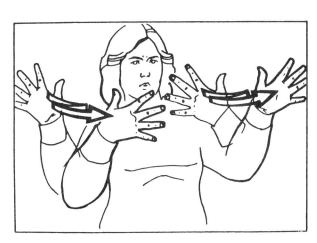

WIND (weather)

WINDOW

WINE

WINTER

WITH (together)

119

WITHOUT

WOMAN

WONDERFUL (fantastic, great)

WORD (<u>vocabulary</u>)

WORK (job)

WORRY

WORSE (multiply)

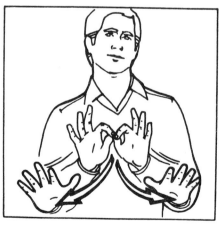

WORTHLESS

WRITE

WRONG (mistake)

X

Y

YEAR

YEAR-FUTURE (next year)

YEAR-PAST (last year)

YELLOW

YES

YESTERDAY

YOU

YOU-ALL

YOU-3

YOU-2

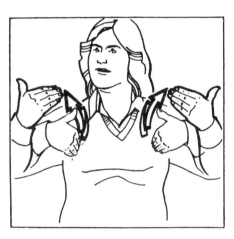

YOUNG (youth)

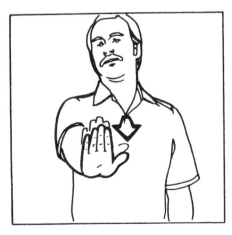

YOUR

YOURSELF (your own)

Z

B·A·S·I·C S·I·G·N COMMUNICATION

COMMUNICATION

NUMBERS

0 (zero)

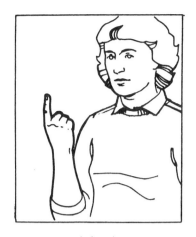

1 (one)

2 (two)

3 (three)

4 (four)

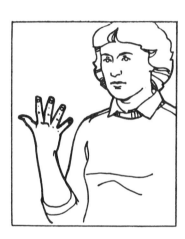

5 (five)

6 (six)

7 (seven)

8 (eight)

9 (nine)

10 (ten)

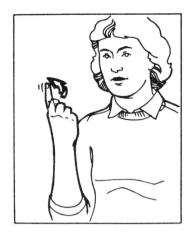

11 (eleven)

12 (twelve)

13 (thirteen)

14 (fourteen)

15 (fifteen)

16 (sixteen)

17 (seventeen)

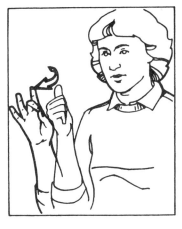

18 (eighteen)

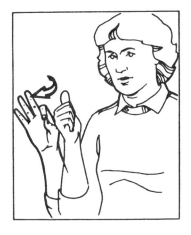

19 (nineteen)

20 (twenty)

21₁ (twenty-one)

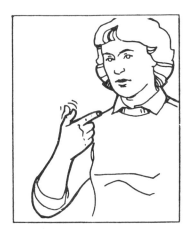

21₂ (twenty-one)

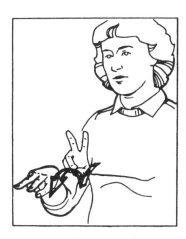

22 (twenty-two)

23 (twenty-three)

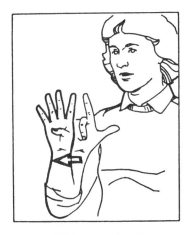

24 (twenty-four)

25 (twenty-five)

127

26 (twenty-six)

27 (twenty-seven)

28 (twenty-eight)

29 (twenty-nine)

30 (thirty)

1-HUNDRED (100)

1-THOUSAND (1,000)

1-MILLION (1,000,000)

1-BILLION (1,000,000,000)

128

ONE-HALF (½)

ONE-THIRD (⅓)

B·A·S·I·C S·I·G·N
COMMUNICATION

CLASSIFIERS

Classifiers

American Sign Language (ASL) has a set of signs which function in a rather unique way. These signs are called classifiers (Bellugi & Newkirk, 1977; Klima & Bellugi, 1979; Supalla, 1978, Baker & Cokely, 1980).

Linguistic analysis of classifiers in ASL is incomplete at this time but we know that there are at least two types of classifiers. The first are classifiers which represent things having certain distinctive characteristics. For example a three-handshape oriented with the thumb pointing up and the first two fingers pointing forward is used to designate the class of land or water vehicles e.g. a car, bus, truck, van, boat, or submarine.

The second type are classifiers that describe the physical characteristics of things and people. These classifiers have been called size and shape specifiers or SASSes. For example, a g-handshape can be used to describe the 'thinness' of an object.

Your instructor will demonstrate some of the specific ways that classifiers are used in signed communication. One important rule for using classifiers is to always clearly name the object, animal, or person for which the classifier will stand. This is similar to how pronouns in English work. Classifiers represent a very potent descriptive force in sign communication and their use is governed by very specific grammatical rules. For further information, it is suggested that you read the references cited above.

In this section classifiers are illustrated. Below each illustration, the caption shows the classifier's gloss. Within parenthesis below each gloss are some examples of the types of things that the classifier can stand for. The words in parenthesis do not define the total set of things for which the classifier can be used but are examples of its uses.

CL:3
(land or water vehicle: car, bus, train, ship, submarine, motorcycle)

CL:F
(small round thin flat objects: buttons, coins, spots, tokens)

CL:Ċ
(larger round thin flat objects: campaign buttons, silver dollars, large cookies)

CL:C̈
(thicker round flat objects: hockey puck, flat round paper weight)

CL:C
(cylindrical objects: cup, bottle, pipe, round post, glass)

CL:1
(thin long things: persons, pencils, poles)

CL:Λ
(legs of a person)

CL:V̈
(small animal: rabbit, bird, squirrel)

CL:5
(mass of something occupying space: buildings, piles of manure, clumps of flowers, cities)

135

CL:Å
(objects occupying space: lamp, block of wood, house)

CL:B
(flat objects: paper, book, floor, ceiling)

CL:G
(thinness: picture frame, book binding, veneer)

CL:C
(thickness: cover of snow, book binding)

B·A·S·I·C S·I·G·N
COMMUNICATION

REFERENCES

References

Baker, C. & Cokely, D. American Sign
    Language: A teachers' resource text on
    grammar and culture. T.J. Publishers,
    1980.

Bellugi, U. & Klima, E. The roots of
    language in the sign talk of the deaf.
    Psychology Today, 1972, June, 61-64,
    76.

Bellugi, U. & Newkirk, D. Formal devices
    for creating new signs in ASL. Proceed-
    ings of the First National Symposium on
    Sign Language Research and Teaching.
    National Association of the Deaf, 1977.

Frishberg, N. Arbitrariness and Iconicity:
    Historical change in American Sign
    Language. Language, 1975, 51 (3),
    696-719.

Klima, E. & Bellugi, U. The Signs of Lan-
    guage. Cambridge, Mass.: Harvard
    University Press, 1979.

Supalla, T. Morphology of verbs of motion
    and location in American Sign Lan-
    guage. Proceedings of the Second Na-
    tional Symposium on Sign Language
    Research and Teaching. National
    Association of the Deaf, 1978.

B·A·S·I·C S·I·G·N
COMMUNICATION

INDEX

A

143

D

E

F

149

I

J

153

P

155

159